TEEN GUIDE TO FIRST JOBS

MANAGING INCOME

by Jenny Crooks-Johnson

BrightPoint Press

San Diego, CA

BrightPoint Press

an imprint of ReferencePoint Press, Inc.
Printed in the United States

For more information, contact:
BrightPoint Press
PO Box 27779
San Diego, CA 92198
www.BrightPointPress.com

LIBRARY OF CONGRESS CATALOGING-IN-PUBLICATION DATA

Name: Crooks-Johnson, Jenny, author.
Title: Managing income / by Jenny Crooks-Johnson.
Description: San Diego, CA: ReferencePoint Press, 2027 | Series: Teen guide to first jobs | Includes bibliographical references and index. | Audience: Grades 7–9
Identifiers: ISBN 9781678214425 (hardcover) | ISBN 9781678214432 (eBook)
The complete Library of Congress record is available at www.loc.gov.

CONTENTS

AT A GLANCE

- Financial goals guide people's spending and savings choices. These goals can be for short-term or long-term needs and wants.

- Turning financial goals into SMART goals makes them easier to complete. SMART stands for specific, measurable, achievable, relevant, and time-bound.

- A budget is a useful planning tool for managing income. Budgets help people make financial decisions. They also keep track of fixed and variable expenses.

- Interest is the cost of borrowing money. Bank customers can earn money from the interest in their savings accounts. Savings and money market accounts usually pay higher interest rates.

- Bank accounts offer safety and ease for managing income. People who keep money in bank accounts can earn interest and other benefits.

- Checking accounts are useful for daily purchases. Savings accounts are useful for long-term purchases or emergencies.

- Making time to review a person's own spending habits is important to keep on track of financial goals. Other good practices include building a list of goals and checking bank statements.

EMMA'S FIRST PAYCHECK

Emma waved goodbye to her last customers. She worked at an ice cream shop. It had been a long workday. But Emma had just completed her first 2 weeks of her job. It was payday.

"Today was busy," said Emma's boss.

"That summer heat brought in a lot of customers," said Emma. "Luckily, Luke is the fastest ice cream scooper around!"

Working a summer job is a great way for teens to gain money and new skills.

"Luke is fast," said her boss. "But you're learning quickly." She handed Emma a check for $520 and a form. "Here's your first paycheck. And here's a form for **direct deposit**. Fill it out if you want your checks to go right into your bank account."

After the store was clean, both Luke and Emma unlocked their bikes.

"First paycheck, right?" asked Luke.

"Yes," said Emma. "A few more of these and I'll be riding home on an e-bike. What about you?"

"I have a goal of saving up $12,000 for welding school. I transfer $300 from each paycheck into my savings account. That's the bank account I place money in to save for future goals. The rest goes into my

Putting spare change into a jar is one way to start saving early.

checking account. That's the bank account I use for everyday purchases."

"Are checking and savings accounts hard to set up?" Emma asked.

"Not really," said Luke. "But you're a minor like me. That means you'll need to go to the bank with your parents to set them up. I had to bring my identification forms.

I also brought some money to put in. The process didn't take very long."

"Thanks," said Emma. It didn't sound hard at all.

That night, Emma thought about her own savings goals. She already knew she wanted to attend college. She calculated that it would be good to save at least $10,000. She also looked into getting her own bank account. The next day, Emma and her parents made an appointment with a bank. Then she went with her parents to set up her savings and checking accounts.

Three days later, Emma handed her boss the direct deposit form. It had her new checking account number. She moved $400 from her checking account into her savings account each month. She was still saving for an e-bike. It would take longer to get than she first thought. But Emma felt good that she had a plan to manage her income.

Talking to an adult can help young people learn more about financial skills.

WHAT IS MANAGING INCOME

Managing income helps people move toward financial goals. People who do not manage their income can overspend. They may not have enough money to meet their money goals. Sometimes an unexpected

Financial goals are a great way to save for future purchases. People might save for education or a shopping trip.

emergency occurs. If a person gets sick or injured, they might need to spend money on medicine. But managing income can help prevent these problems. People won't always need to worry about unexpected costs. People who manage their income know what they need to spend money on.

A budget is a useful planning tool for managing income. It helps people make smart financial decisions. Budgets also keep track of different expenses. Banks are other useful resources for managing income. They provide helpful benefits, such as a place to store money. Budgets and banks can help teens build good spending and saving habits. Teens can learn how to manage their income while completing their financial goals.

CHAPTER ONE

FINANCIAL GOALS

It is easy for people to spend money without planning on it. This habit can lead to using too much money. Financial plans help people to spend money on what they most value. A financial plan can help with setting goals. These goals motivate people to save money, which makes it easier to follow a financial plan.

People who save money in bank accounts can earn interest. Interest is the

Spending too much money can stop people from achieving their future financial goals. Even small purchases can add up.

cost of borrowing money. Bank customers can earn money from the interest in their savings. Banks pay interest as a reward. They allow other people to borrow the money in a person's bank account. This is called a loan. People use loans to buy houses and cars. People with loans pay interest to the bank. And the bank pays some of this interest to the person it

Compound Interest

Compound interest is earning interest on interest. A person who puts money into a bank account will earn a percentage of interest on that money. This increases the amount of money they have. The next month, they will have even more money to earn interest on. This will earn them even more interest.

borrowed money from. Interest earnings help teens reach their financial goals faster.

Georgia I. Lainiotis is a financial expert. She's the author of *Personal Finance for Teens and Young Adults.* She said, "When

Learning to save money can help teens build lifelong skills. These include managing money or other resources to reach a goal.

it comes to savings, small steps add up with time. The amount you decide to save is up to you and depends on your personal goals and earnings."[1] Even small amounts of savings and interest can make larger goals possible. Financial goals are for both short-term and long-term goals. They also include both needs and wants.

MAKING FINANCIAL GOALS

Financial goals for a person's needs are important. Needs are must-haves for everyday living. These include food, shelter, and basic clothing. Having money for emergencies is also important. An example might be paying to have a bike or car repaired. Wants are nice to have. These purchases could include video games,

Making a list of goals is a helpful way to keep track of future purchases. People can list them on paper, phones, or computers.

hobbies, and movie tickets. Needs and wants are different from person to person.

Short-term and long-term goals are important to note as well. Short-term goals are focused on the next 1 to 3 years. Teens could be saving money for a concert ticket or bike. Long-term goals are for purchases further into the future. This could be 5 years or more. Teens might want to save money for trade school or to rent an apartment.

Talking with friends about financial goals is a great way to learn more about ways to save and spend. Friends can help each other keep on track of their goals.

People usually don't have enough money for all of their goals. Because of this, it is helpful to rank goals. This allows people to focus on saving for specific things first. Then they can tackle other goals later.

SMART FINANCIAL GOALS

SMART goals make savings and future purchases easier to complete. SMART stands for specific, measurable, achievable, **relevant**, and time-bound. Specific means the goal is targeted and focused. Measurable means the goal can be tracked, such as earning a certain amount of money. Emma's goal to save $10,000 for college is specific and measurable.

An achievable goal is realistic for a person's situation. A relevant goal is one

Saving money can take a long time. It is important to celebrate financial goals once they are achieved.

that feels important to a person's current life. And a time-bound goal has a specific target date. Emma's summer paycheck is about $500 every 2 weeks. Emma's goal is to save $10,000 for college in three summers. Her goal is realistic, relevant, and time-bound.

Hanna Newman is a recent college graduate. Her teen job was clearing tables at a restaurant. She set a goal to earn $9,000 every summer for college housing. “I didn’t want to feel stressed about earning rent money while I was taking college classes,” said Hanna. “So, I deposited all the money from my paychecks into my savings account until I met my goal. My spending money came from my tips.”[2] Setting financial goals is an important first step toward managing income.

CHAPTER TWO

BUDGETS

Budgets are important parts of a financial plan. A budget keeps track of income and expenses over time. It helps make financial plans more achievable. Budgets also help people review their money habits. This lets people know where they need to cut spending.

Charles Schwab is a financial company. It did an online survey of 1,000 adults of all ages across the United States. It reported

Starting a budgeting plan can help teens build good money tracking habits.

that "only 36 percent of Americans have a written financial plan. Among those who do, three in four say it makes them feel more in control of their finances and nearly all

Teens gain new skills when they start a job. These skills are just as important as their paycheck.

(96 percent) say they feel confident that they will reach their financial goals."[3]

AVERAGE MONTHLY INCOME

The first step in budgeting is to calculate monthly income. Income may change from month to month. Teens may get side jobs. These could include babysitting, pet care, or graphic design work. Teens may get two paychecks one month and three paychecks the next. Calculating an average monthly income can provide the number for a budget.

To calculate average income, people first need a record of all their income. They can use their personal records for this data. Bank statements are another helpful record of income. These track

Some banks send electronic bank statements instead of paper statements. This allows people to look at a summary of their transactions as they happen.

every money transaction for an account. Transactions include deposits. This is when money is added to an account. They also include withdrawals. This is when money is taken out of an account.

EXPENSES

Some monthly expenses stay mostly the same. These are called fixed expenses. Rent is an example of a fixed expense. Monthly savings toward a goal could also be a fixed expense. Other expenses change a lot. These are called variable expenses. Luke might have a category in his budget called entertainment. This could include money he spends going out with friends. He might spend $50 in entertainment in a single month. The next month he might spend $100. For Luke, entertainment is a variable expense.

Variable expenses can be hard to budget for because they change. But calculating a monthly average of these expenses helps. Luke has 3 months of records. His average

It is important to keep track of variable expenses, such as groceries and gas payments.

budget is $75 for entertainment. Many people like to use yearly averages for greater detail. People can estimate their expenses, too. Then they can update their budget when they have more complete numbers.

SAMPLE COLLEGE OR TRADE SCHOOL STUDENT BUDGET

Monthly Income	Income
Student Job	$450
Money from Savings	$1,975
Total Income	$2,425
Monthly Fixed Expenses	**Expenses**
Rent	$700
Utilities	$50
Phone Plan	$40
Tuition Payment	$1,000
Books and Supplies	$100
Bus Pass	$40
Total Fixed Expenses	$1,930
Monthly Variable Expenses	**Expenses**
Groceries	$300
Dining Out	$30
Fun with Friends	$50
Hobbies	$25
Personal Care	$40
Miscellaneous Items	$50
Total Variable Expenses	$495
Total Fixed + Variable Expenses	**$2,425**

This chart provides an example of a student budgeting for a year with $16,000 saved in their bank account. It shows both fixed and variable expenses.

BALANCING A BUDGET

A balanced budget is when a person does not spend more money than they earned in income. A balanced budget has enough money for needed expenses. One way to balance a budget is to earn more income. Teens can take on extra work shifts. They can work overtime or get a side job. These additional sources of income allow teens to gain more money.

Teens can also balance their budgets by reducing the amount they spend. They can find low-cost ways to use their money. For example, they can use discounts when shopping. They can buy used goods. But it is important to keep some money for wants in a budget. This allows people to enjoy their earnings and still manage their income.

Teens might work more than one job. It is important to balance work and school to prevent burnout.

Buying used clothes is one way to save money.

There are different kinds of budget plans. One popular plan is the 50/30/20 budget. This budget plan is easy to follow. People limit spending on their needs to 50 percent of their total income. Then they use 30 percent for their wants. The 20 percent is used for savings. The 50/30/20 budget is useful for focusing on needs and savings.

Another budget plan is the reverse budget. This plan reverses the budgeting process. People pay themselves first. They put aside a certain amount of money from their paycheck into their savings goal. Then they divide the rest of their paycheck between their needs and wants. No matter the plan, budgeting is an important income management tool.

Many Types of Budgeting Plans

There are many ways to budget. The envelope system is a way of budgeting physical cash. People place paper money in different labeled envelopes. They store money for future purchases. The zero-based budget is a plan that makes sure that savings and expenses total zero. This budget is ideal for people who are very detailed based. They make sure every dollar is being used.

CHAPTER THREE

BANK ACCOUNTS

Bank accounts are helpful tools for managing money. People with bank accounts can deposit their paychecks directly into their accounts for free. Without bank accounts, people must cash paychecks at their employer's bank. Or they must pay a fee to cash the check at a store.

Bank accounts offer a safe place to keep money. The US Federal Deposit Insurance Corporation (FDIC) insures the safety of

Banks are places where people can keep money safe. People can also store important documents in a safe deposit box at a bank.

Portofino Realty Advisors
WELLS FARGO
24 MINUTE PARKING
Y174
6484

money in banks. A bank could burn down or go **bankrupt**. But the FDIC will replace up to $250,000 that a person keeps in the bank if it does. The FDIC will do this for each bank a customer has money in. The FDIC website says, "Opening a bank account can be one of the most important

Some banking apps allow people to transfer money to other people.

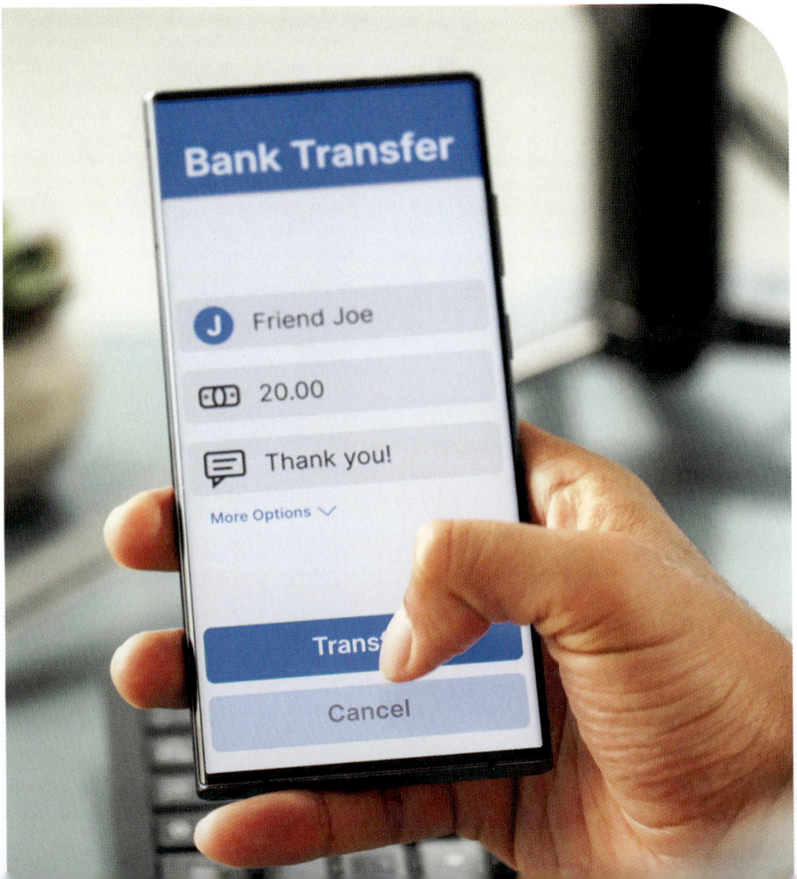

steps you take toward reaching your financial goals."[4]

Banks offer useful services, too. These include online banking tools and phone apps. These tools help people make transactions without going to the bank. People can pay bills electronically. They can also check their **account balances**.

CHECKING ACCOUNTS

A checking account is what most people use to spend money. People can write paper checks to pay for items. They can also use debit cards. These are plastic cards linked to a person's checking account that allow for cashless payment.

People can withdraw cash from their checking accounts at banks. They can

ATMs can be found in banks, gas stations, and stores.

also get cash from an **automated** teller machine (ATM). People do not have to pay a fee to use their own bank's ATM. But if they use another bank's ATM, a small service fee may be charged. People will have to keep this in mind when they choose a bank.

Checking accounts may require a minimum balance. They may also charge a fee. This happens when the amount of money in an account falls below the minimum balance. Banks also charge a fee for overdrawing an account. Overdrawing is taking out more money than is in the account. Banks use a system called ChexSystems to track people who have a habit of overdrawing. These people usually have a harder time getting bank accounts. Student checking accounts can be good options for teens. They usually have lower fees and balance requirements.

Some banks also pay interest on checking account balances. A bank lists its **interest rate** as an annual percentage yield (APY). This is the total amount of interest

Banks offer many different services. People can check banks' websites to see which option works best for them.

a person will get on their bank deposits in 1 year.

SAVINGS ACCOUNTS

Savings accounts are ideal for money stored for long-term financial goals. People tend to make fewer withdrawals from their savings accounts. Savings also tend to have higher account balances and interest rates. This means savings usually earn more interest. Savings accounts that pay the highest interest often have higher balance requirements. People can compare banks' interest rates on their websites.

McKay Lyman attends high school in Wyoming. This past summer he had his first job. He moved watering pipes and did weeding on a ranch. McKay says:

I deposited 60 percent of my paychecks into my savings account. I plan to use that money for a future service opportunity, college, and hopefully some kind of car, too. Right now, my savings account only pays .03 percent interest. But as I save more money, I plan to look into savings accounts that pay higher interest rates.[5]

MONEY MARKET ACCOUNTS

Money market accounts combine the benefits of checking and savings accounts. Banks **invest** a part of deposits from these accounts into the US money market. The US money market is where organizations buy and sell short-term investments. These organizations include banks and

Banks can answer financial questions someone might have. People can set up an appointment to discuss different banking plans and options.

Some phones allow people to pay electronically by connecting their bank information to their device.

the government. Banks often earn more interest on these investments than they do on their regular loans. This means money market accounts usually pay higher interest rates than regular savings accounts do.

People can access money in these accounts by using checks, a debit card, or an ATM. But there are often limits on the number of withdrawals each month.

Money market accounts tend to have higher balance requirements as well.

Bank accounts are key tools for managing income. They help people meet their financial goals. Banks can help people track their savings and spending, too. Teens who manage their own bank accounts are learning an important life skill.

Credit Unions

Credit unions offer similar accounts as banks. But credit unions are nonprofit organizations. Profit is another name for income. Credit unions return their income to their customers. Some credit unions offer higher interest rates and lower fees. Most credit unions have membership requirements. Some credit unions are just for teachers or members of the military. Credit unions also tend to have fewer locations and services than banks.

CHAPTER FOUR

STAYING ON TRACK

Life is full of expenses. It's easy to forget about financial goals. People might not stay within their budgets. They might not remember to review bank account transactions. People who do not check their accounts may overdraw. They may pay extra fees. These habits can make it hard to afford different needs and wants.

Learning to track and review money builds strong financial skills. It helps people

Building strong financial habits early on is important.

manage their income. When people track and review their transactions, it helps keep them on budget. It also helps them move toward their financial goals. This tracking takes time, but it is worth it. The US Bank says, "Developing sound financial habits early on can have lifelong benefits, from better quality of life to stronger personal relationships."[6]

TRACKING

People can track their income, spending, and savings on paper. They can record what they earn and spend in a journal. Some people use their phones or laptops, too. Writing down when money is spent is a good way for people to stay within their budget. Even small purchases can add up.

For example, buying a six-dollar drink a few times a week can feel fine. But it can soon add up to more than $900 in a year.

Many people use apps to track spending. These apps pull account information from a person's bank. They can also pull spending

Some people might feel overwhelmed by tracking. It can help to focus on tracking two or three categories that a person tends to overspend in.

data from credit cards. Credit cards are another way to make daily purchases. Credit is money people agree to borrow and pay later, usually with interest. If people do not pay their credit card balance each month, then credit card companies loan

Some banking apps show graphs that break down a person's spendings.

them money. However, people must pay high interest rates on their credit card balance.

Apps can put expenses into budget categories. The app then alerts people when they've overspent in a category. Apps can also show progress towards savings goals. Some apps are free. Other apps cost money. Many bank apps have money tracking and budgeting tools built in. These are free for their customers to use.

People can also track their transactions by reviewing bank statements. Many people upload their banking and credit card data to a spreadsheet on a computer or phone. They use it to track their spending and savings. Keeping receipts from cash purchases can also be important.

People can add them to spreadsheets or apps to track these purchases.

REVIEWING

People should choose a regular time to review their spending habits, goals,

Teens can review transactions with an adult to make sure they are correct.

and budgets. A weekly review may work for some people. They may compare the past week's spending with their budget. If they've overspent, they can make plans to spend less the next week.

Budgets and plans don't always work the first time. They may need to change. A weekly review is a good time to notice spending trends. A person can note where they spend too much money. They can also celebrate progress made toward goals. This helps people stay motivated to keep going.

Claire Johnson is a high school junior. Her first job is at a clothing store. Claire says, "I want to save about $14,000 for college, so I use my bank app every couple weeks to check my spending and see how much I've saved. If I spend too much one month, I'll cut back the next month, like maybe I'll go out to eat with friends less."[7]

Creating SMART financial goals, setting up a budget, and using bank accounts are all important steps to manage income. People who make it a habit to track and review their budgets are more likely to

Checking for Fraud

Checking bank statements can help people spot errors. A person may call their bank if they notice any mistakes. Reviewing statements can also help people spot **fraudulent** transactions. These are criminal transactions that a person did not make themselves. Government laws protect a person from errors or fraud. These laws require banks to return a person's money if the bank made an error or if a purchase was fraudulent. However, people should let their bank know of these problems as soon as possible.

make progress toward their financial goals. Earning income at a young age is an exciting financial step. Managing income takes time and practice. But it can lead to financial security and peace of mind.

GLOSSARY

account balances

the total amount of money in someone's bank accounts

automated

operated without thought

bankrupt

when a person or business does not have enough money to pay the amount they owe

direct deposit

an electronic payment of money from an employer or other source into an account

fraudulent

wrongful or criminal actions to receive financial gain

interest rate

the percentage of money a financial institution pays on account balances

invest

to give money to a person or business with the expectation of earning income or profit

relevant

related to the matter at hand

SOURCE NOTES

CHAPTER ONE: FINANCIAL GOALS

1. Georgia I. Lainiotis, *Personal Finance for Teens and Young Adults*. Dgil Global Ventures LLC, 2023, p. 11.

2. Hanna Newman, Personal interview, October 2, 2025.

CHAPTER TWO: BUDGETS

3. Quoted in "Charles Schwab Modern Wealth Survey 2024," *Charles Schwab*, 2024. www.aboutschwab.com.

CHAPTER THREE: BANK ACCOUNTS

4. Quoted in "Top Reasons to #GetBanked," *FDIC*, April 2021. www.fdic.gov.

5. McKay Lyman, Personal interview, September 30, 2025.

CHAPTER FOUR: STAYING ON TRACK

6. Quoted in "Family Finances," *US Bank*, n.d. www.usbank.com.

7. Claire Johnson, Personal interview, October 5, 2025.

FOR FURTHER RESEARCH

BOOKS

Jean Chatzky and Kathryn Tuggle, *How to Money: Your Ultimate Visual Guide to the Basics of Finance*. Roaring Brook Press, 2022.

Sue Bradford Edwards, *Succeeding at Your First Job*. BrightPoint Press, 2027.

Jenny Crooks-Johnson, *Quick Guide to Living on a Budget.* BrightPoint Press, 2025.

INTERNET SOURCES

Kate Rockwood, "Banking 101: Understanding How Banks Work," *Step,* October 11, 2023. https://step.com.

"Making a Budget," *Consumer.gov*, August 2024. https://consumer.gov.

"The Best Financial Goals Examples for Students," *Centier Bank*, October 2, 2023. www.centier.com.

WEBSITES

Get Banked!

www.fdic.gov

The FDIC page offers resources for learning more about banks. This includes opening a bank account and managing income.

How Money Smart Are you?

https://playmoneysmart.fdic.gov

The FDIC is a government agency that oversees financial institutions. This suite of resources includes fourteen games to help educate people on financial skills.

Young AmeriTowne

https://yacenter.org

Young AmeriTowne is a nonprofit youth financial education center in Colorado. They offer in-person financial experiences and free online money matters classes. They also have Young Americans Bank, which is a real FDIC-insured bank designed for youth.

INDEX

IMAGE CREDITS

Cover: © Pixel-Shot/Shutterstock Images
5: © Rodica Vasiliev/Shutterstock Images
7: © OP Digital Solutions/Shutterstock Images
9: © Pixel-Shot/Shutterstock Images
11: © Dragon Images/Shutterstock Images
12: © LightField Studios/Shutterstock Images
15: © Trzykropy/Shutterstock Images
17: © Inside Creative House/Shutterstock Images
19: © Prostock-Studio/Shutterstock Images
20: © Alfons Moles Juny/Shutterstock Images
22: © Andrii Lemelianenko/Shutterstock Images
25: © fizkes/Shutterstock Images
26: © Iryna Inshyna/Shutterstock Images
28: © Andrey_Popov/Shutterstock Images
30: © BearFotos/Shutterstock Images
31: Red Line Editorial
33: © Mishchenko Svitlana/Shutterstock Images
34: © Chay_Tee/Shutterstock Images
37: © Leonard Zhukovsky/Shutterstock Images
38: © Andrey_Popov/Shutterstock Images
40: © VisualProduction/Shutterstock Images
42: © Prostock-Studio/Shutterstock Images
45: © vk_st/Shutterstock Images
46: © PeopleImages/Shutterstock Images
49: © Rodica Vasiliev/Shutterstock Images
51: © Odua Images/Shutterstock Images
52: © Andrey_Popov/Shutterstock Images
54: © Miljan Zivkovic/Shutterstock Images

ABOUT THE AUTHOR

Jenny Crooks-Johnson is an author who loves to write fiction and nonfiction books for young people. She lives in Colorado with her family. She's grateful to all the youth who let her interview them for this book. Keep making the best financial decisions you can. It will pay off in so many ways!